THE ACADEMIC YEAR ... strange time for freedo... United States. Despite the continued strength of the First Amendment's legal protections for unpopular speech, stories about individuals (famous or otherwise) caught saying something offensive to someone or some group have become a media obsession. It seems as if every day brings a new controversy regarding the purportedly offensive remarks of a celebrity, an official, or an ordinary citizen, followed by irate calls for the speaker to suffer some sort of retribution.

In the spring of 2014, recordings of racist remarks by Los Angeles Clippers owner Donald Sterling dominated CNN coverage for months, inspiring public outrage that likely will result in Sterling's losing his basketball franchise. Not long before that, the controversy of the day involved Phil Robertson, the patriarch of A&E's popular television show *Duck Dynasty*, for making insulting remarks about homosexuals and African Americans. That incident was preceded by the fall of

Paula Deen, whose career collapsed (perhaps temporarily) after she admitted to having used a racial epithet at some undefined time decades in the past. The list of celebrities who have made headlines for allegedly offensive statements seems to be ever expanding; high-profile offenders include Gary Oldman, Don Imus, Mel Gibson, Jerry Seinfeld, Isaiah Washington, and Alec Baldwin.

Oftentimes, the speakers are not merely vilified but even lose their jobs over their comments. Juan Williams at NPR, Rick Sanchez and Roland Martin at CNN, and Martin Bashir and (again) Alec Baldwin at MSNBC all lost their media positions because of controversial remarks. Admittedly, many of the offending comments were not particularly sympathetic, but the public's appetite for punishing attempts at candor gone wrong, drunken rants, or even private statements made in anger or frustration seems to be growing at an alarming rate.

Even satirical comedian Stephen Colbert ran afoul of the speech police when he made

> *The public's appetite for punishing attempts at candor gone wrong, drunken rants, or even private statements made in anger or frustration seems to be growing at an alarming rate.*

a joke on his show that used racial insensitivity to mock racial insensitivity. The #Cancel-Colbert movement quickly picked up steam but ultimately did more to produce Twitter chatter than to threaten the career of the popular comedian. It did, however, shine a light on the thought pattern of the modern American censor: there must be zero tolerance for anything that anyone might consider offensive, regardless of the context.

And then there was the case of the Mozilla Corporation's Brendan Eich, who was pressured to resign from his brief stint as the company's CEO after it re-emerged that he had donated $1,000 to the campaign for California's Proposition 8, a ballot initiative opposing same-sex marriage, back in 2008. The Eich incident was troubling on many levels. Not only did it demonstrate a surprisingly short national memory – until fairly recently, the majority of Americans opposed gay marriage, including both President Obama and Hillary Clinton – but it also seemed to indicate that some religious or social conservatives would have to choose between their beliefs and their professions. Eich's coerced resignation sent such a disquieting message that a coalition of 58 gay-rights activists, scholars, columnists, and pundits across the ideological spectrum signed a statement titled "Freedom to Marry, Freedom to Dissent: Why We Must Have Both." The statement warned that the Eich case "signal[ed] an eagerness by some supporters of same-sex marriage to punish rather than to criticize or to persuade those who disagree."

Some argued that the Eich incident was

not about "free speech," because free speech binds only governments and does not prevent private employers from firing employees (or encouraging them to step down) based on their beliefs. This argument is incorrect. It's true that what happened to Eich was not an actual First Amendment violation, but that does not mean it had nothing to do with free speech.

Though often used interchangeably, the concept of freedom of speech and the First Amendment are not the same thing. While the First Amendment protects freedom of speech and freedom of the press as they relate to duties of the state and state power, freedom of speech is a far broader idea that includes additional cultural values. These values incorporate healthy intellectual habits, such as giving the other side a fair hearing, reserving judgment, tolerating opinions that offend or anger us, believing that everyone is entitled to his or her own opinion, and recognizing that even people whose points of view we find repugnant might be (at least partially) right. At the heart of these values is epistemic humility — a fancy way of saying that we must always keep in mind that we could be wrong or, at least, that we can always learn something from listening to the other side. Free speech as a cultural value will be my primary concern in this Broadside, not the state of First Amendment jurisprudence. And the national obsession with punishing jokes, rants, drunken tirades, and even deeply held beliefs shows a growing hostility toward free speech as a cultural value.

Given this climate, it is unsurprising that American higher education, where unpopular speech has been restricted for decades, has earned media attention for being especially intolerant in the past year. My organization, the Foundation for Individual Rights in Education (FIRE), which exists to combat violations of student and faculty free speech and other constitutional rights, has been busier than ever in 2013-14. In this Broadside, I will be discussing at length recent campus incidents and trends, including "disinvitation season" (the increased push by faculty and students to disinvite guest speakers on campus) and the emergence of demands for "trigger warnings" (written and/or spoken warnings to students that books, films, or other course material might be emotionally upsetting) on campus.

But those examples are just two symptoms of an academic environment that has long been souring on robust free speech and expression. Alan Charles Kors and Harvey Silverglate extensively exposed the rise of speech codes and political correctness on campus in their 1998 book *The Shadow University: The Betrayal of Liberty on America's Campuses*, and I updated and built upon their work in my 2012 book *Unlearning Liberty: Campus Censorship and the End of American Debate*. In *Unlearning Liberty*, I argued:

> *Administrators [on campus] have been able to convince well-meaning students to accept outright censorship by creating the impression that freedom of speech is somehow the enemy of social*

progress. When students began leaving college with that lesson under their belts, it was only a matter of time before the cultivation of bad intellectual habits on campus started harming the dialogue of our entire country. The tactics and attitudes that shut down speech on campus are bleeding into the larger society and wreaking havoc on the way we talk among ourselves.

I continue to believe that the increased national focus on punishing offensive speech stems, in large part, from the "bleeding out" of the bad intellectual habits of American higher education. However, I do not think – nor have I ever thought – that blame for the erosion of support for the cultural value of freedom of speech can be laid entirely on the ivory tower. The "It's all academia's fault" argument does not adequately explain why freedom of speech seems to be on the decline across the globe, even in countries that claim to value civil and political rights.

The suppression of "offensive" speech is

very common outside the U.S., and it often occurs in countries that seemingly share the classical-liberal tradition. In April 2014, a British politician was arrested for "religious/racial harassment" after delivering a speech in which he approvingly quoted a passage from a book by Winston Churchill that disparaged the Islamic faith and its adherents. Censorship in general is on the rise in the U.K., from the jailing of people caught making "grossly offensive" comments on social media to the banning of R&B singer Robin Thicke's hit song "Blurred Lines" by student unions at more than 20 British universities. In February 2013, the interior minister of Iceland – a country that views itself as very socially progressive – crafted legislation to ban online pornography.

Furthermore, Europe has recently seen the spread of the doctrine of the "right to be forgotten." The European Court of Justice ruled in May 2014 that search engines like Google are required to remove links from their search results at the request of private parties to whom the information pertains unless the companies can present a public-interest justification for leaving the links active. Both this vague standard and the odd incentive structure it creates (relying on Yahoo and Google to spend money to defend individual articles and links) threaten the freedom of the press and the public's freedom to access information. In July 2014, for example, Google deleted from its search results three articles from the *Guardian* about a retired Scottish soccer referee who once "lied about his reasons for granting a penalty kick." Complying with the European Court's ruling, Google decided that because the referee had since retired, he was no longer a public figure and thus his right to privacy now trumped the public's right to know about his involvement in the incident. It is hard to understand why the public's right to access information about a scandal should expire once the responsible party retires from public life.

Elsewhere, India — the world's largest democracy — has asked Google and Facebook to screen user content for "disparaging" or "inflammatory" postings, thereby taking yet another step in a national movement to suppress speech that author Salman Rushdie has called a "cultural emergency." Meanwhile, Turkey has overachieved in the censorship realm, with its law forbidding criticism of Mustafa Kemal Ataturk (the founder of modern Turkey), its law forbidding insults to the Turkish nation, its temporary implementation of a nationwide block on access to Twitter and YouTube, and its prime minister's practice of warning the news media not to publish "insults" against him.

People all over the globe are coming to expect emotional and intellectual comfort as though it were a right.

The "It's all academia's fault" argument cannot explain these developments, nor can it explain why higher education, which is an institution that relies on being a "marketplace of ideas," would turn against free speech in the first place. I believe we are facing a long-term threat to freedom of speech that is much more substantial than the expansion of "liberal groupthink" or "political correctness" from campus.

The increased calls for sensitivity-based censorship represent the dark side of what are otherwise several positive developments for human civilization. As I will explain in the next section, I believe that we are not passing through some temporary phase in which an out-of-touch and hypersensitive elite attempts – and often fails – to impose its speech-restrictive norms on society. It's worse than that: people all over the globe are coming to expect emotional and intellectual comfort as though it were a right. This is precisely what you would expect when you train a generation to believe that they have a right not to be offended. Eventually, they stop demanding freedom *of* speech and start demanding freedom *from* speech.

To be crystal clear, I am in no way absolving higher education of its culpability in exacerbating the movement against free speech. Higher education deserves profound criticism for maintaining and promoting illiberal and unconstitutional speech codes and punishing students and faculty for what they say. However, I believe the even greater failure of higher education is neglecting to teach the intellectual habits that promote debate and discussion, tolerance for views we hate, epistemic humility, and genuine pluralism. I will spend most of the following pages discussing how the rise of "disinvitation season" on campus and the mounting calls for "trigger warnings" represent an increasingly suffocating environment for speech on campus.

If, as I suspect, this push for freedom *from* speech is something like a predictable and natural (if pernicious) force, the single institution that could be doing the most to combat it is higher education, both within and out-side the United States. Unfortunately, far from teaching the intellectual discipline that welcomes a free and robust exchange of ideas, campuses are actively accelerating the push for freedom from speech.

"PROBLEMS OF COMFORT":
WHY WE CAN EXPECT THE THREATS
TO FREE SPEECH TO GET WORSE

We live in what is likely the most peaceful and nonviolent period in human history. Psychologist Steven Pinker made this argument thoroughly and eloquently in his 2011 book *The Better Angels of Our Nature: Why Violence Has Declined*, which compares not only the rates of violence but also the harshness (e.g., public celebrations of torture, animal cruelty, and execution) of previous eras with those of today. The evidence keeps stacking up that the average person's likelihood of dying violently has never been lower.

Meanwhile, more medications than ever are available for the treatment of physical pain, illness, and psychological ailments. The daily presence of disease, discomfort, back-breaking labor, and violence that existed long before the advent of aspirin or antibiotics is hard for us to imagine, but that reality shaped the way previous generations of individuals, religious leaders, and philosophers thought about life.

We also have a greater ability to move from neighborhood to neighborhood, from state to state, or even from country to country than any previous generation. One might imagine that this freedom would lead to the widespread dissemination of different viewpoints. However, as books like Bill Bishop's *The Big Sort: Why the Clustering of Like-Minded America Is Tearing Us Apart* (2008) and Charles Murray's *Coming Apart: The State of White America, 1960-2010* (2012) have demonstrated, we are increasingly using our mobility to congregate within counties, towns, and even neighborhoods populated by politically like-minded people.

Wanting to live in communities that reflect our values is an understandable and very human impulse. However, since it decreases the likelihood – and the accompanying discomfort – of communicating across deep philosophical, religious, or political divides, such self-sorting comes with serious downsides. The social science of what happens when like-minded people talk only among themselves is quite striking: those who are broken up into groups with similar beliefs tend to become more extreme in their opinions and less able to understand the views of those who disagree with them. And psychologists and social scientists such as Jonathan Haidt have found that this polarization is a growing part of the American culture. Many of the resources available to us in the Internet age are further exacerbating the problem. We can now obtain the majority of our information from niche media sources that are specifically tailored to reinforce our existing worldviews, and we can easily converse with those who share our opinions while avoiding or even ganging up on those who do not.

There's no doubt that having an abundance of options and greater physical comfort than we have ever enjoyed as a species is a good thing, but it comes with consequences. These are what I call problems of comfort: the kinds of challenges that get more severe not only *while* other things are getting better but in large part *because* other things are getting better. Obesity is the paradigmatic example of a problem of comfort. This epidemic, with its many negative health effects, is a predictable result of an overabundance of fatty and sugar-rich food. Today's technology, pharmaceuticals, advanced medical care, and limitless sources of cheap calories would be considered unimaginably wonderful by, say, Stone Age human beings. Yet I sincerely doubt that our ancestors would envy our self-obsession, our fearfulness, or our lack of preparedness for adversity.

This lack of readiness is quite understandable. A society in which people can avoid physical pain comparatively easily will produce people who are less prepared to deal with it. Similarly, an environment in which people can easily avoid emotional and intellectual pain will produce people who are less prepared to deal with and are more intolerant toward harsh disagreement, objectionable words, and differing perspectives.

We are instinctively drawn to increased

comfort and decreased pain. The same instinct is driving our rising desire for intellectual comfort, by which I mean a yearning to live in a relatively harmonious environment that does not present thorny intellectual challenges, and in which disagreement is downplayed or avoided altogether.

Unfortunately, far from teaching the intellectual discipline that welcomes a free and robust exchange of ideas, campuses are actively accelerating the push for freedom from speech.

But intellectual comfort is as dangerous as it is seductive.

First of all, placing a premium on intellectual comfort is at odds with the three great pillars of the modern world that Jonathan

Rauch discussed in his 1993 masterpiece *Kindly Inquisitors: The New Attacks on Free Thought.* These pillars are democracy (how we determine who gets to wield legitimate state power), capitalism (how we determine the allocation of wealth), and the intellectual system that Rauch dubbed liberal science (how we determine what is true). As Rauch put it, liberal science is the idea that the "checking of each by each through public criticism is the only legitimate way to decide who is right." Such checking and criticism cannot occur without creating intellectual discomfort. In fact, all three pillars rely on competition – often fierce competition – which, by nature, is not particularly comfortable. For liberal science to thrive, it must take place in an environment where the right to dissent is protected – an environment of free speech and inquiry.

Settling conflicts with discourse and reason rather than wars or duels has been one of the greatest sources of peace and prosperity in human history. But make no mistake about it: we are still at combat with one another. We simply use words instead of weapons to determine who gets to wield power and decide what is considered to be true. In such high-stakes matters, it should come as no surprise that our dialogue can (and perhaps *should*) be heated, passionate, and often disquieting. But the idea that we can truly tackle hard issues while remaining universally inoffensive – an impossible pipe dream even if it were desirable – seems to be growing increasingly popular.

Safeguarding intellectual comfort is also at odds with scientific and cultural advancement. Science teaches us to be wary of "confirmation bias," our tendency to be receptive to only the evidence that confirms our point of view. Humans excel at believing that we are right without verifying our beliefs. There is a very good reason that it took so long for the scientific method to catch on; the idea of testing our assumptions and following what experimentation tells us, even if the results contradict our most basic beliefs, is counterintuitive, in the most literal sense. Applying this method to important personal or societal issues can be particularly upsetting. If we refuse to accept this intellectual discomfort and instead embrace complacency and certainty, we fall victim to confirmation bias, and progress inevitably stalls.

As people come to expect intellectual comfort, some will increasingly demand that the world conform to their expectations. Others will simply avoid political and intellectual discussions or even comedy and satire that they find disquieting. Such reactions dull the exchange of ideas and cement polarization. Worse still are those who come to see themselves as defenders of the feelings of others, even when such help is not requested or desired. As I discuss in *Unlearning Liberty*, these self-righteous censors often construct a "hero narrative" about themselves in which they are morally pure crusaders who must protect society from the objectionable opinions of the unenlightened masses.

The quest for intellectual comfort is almost as inevitable as the quest for physical comfort. We cannot expect people to want less of either in the future. However, the pursuit of increased intellectual comfort, with its accompanying expectation that others should confirm our views, is deeply harmful to intellectual, political, and scientific progress. (I also believe it's harmful to individual happiness and personal growth, but that's a topic for another book.)

As readers can already tell, I am approaching this topic from a more fundamental standpoint than the liberal-vs.-conservative or progressive-vs.-conservative perspective that is common in culture-war discussions. Among the many problems of the left-vs.-right approach is the fact that it necessarily oversimplifies highly complex issues. I have made no bones about the fact that campus censorship is largely motivated by people from the political left. At the same time, I know that there are conservatives who oppose freedom of speech and the right to engage in offensive, blasphemous, or sexually explicit expression. And many on the left side of the spectrum, such as Nadine Strossen, Wendy Kaminer, Nat Hentoff, Floyd Abrams, and Glenn Greenwald, are true free-speech purists. If we characterize the push toward censorship as a phenomenon that comes from only the left, we automatically let half the population off the hook and demonize the other half, many of whom may potentially be allies in the fight for free speech.

I will, however, acknowledge one aspect of the standard American political divide that has great relevance to the rest of this Broadside. In his excellent 2012 book *The Righteous Mind: Why Good People Are Divided by Politics and Religion*, Jonathan Haidt explored the foundations of human morality and tried to determine how they cohere and from where they originate. He concluded that political conservatives have multiple sources for their moral norms that include the values of traditional societies around the world, such as sacredness, loyalty, and respect for authority. In contrast, Haidt wrote, American liberals and progressives primarily emphasize the "care ethic," whereby one's analysis of the morality of an issue begins and ends with whether or not the proposed action demonstrates care for the well-being or feelings of others, with particular focus on the needs of a relatively large category of people defined as "victims." As progressive author and professor George Lakoff put it in *The Political Mind*, "Behind every progressive policy lies a single moral value: empathy." Lakoff's assertion lends support to Haidt's argument that progressive morality is largely one-dimensional, driven primarily by the care ethic. If true, this theory does an excellent job of explaining why the push for sensitivity-based censorship increasingly comes from the left wing of the political spectrum. Whichever portion of the spectrum emphasizes care above all other values will be more sympathetic to attempts to prevent offensive or challenging speech and to provide those they view as vulnerable with as much freedom *from* speech as possible.

Campus Speech, Disinvitation Season, and the Movement From the "Right Not to Be Offended" to the "Expectation of Confirmation"

While I believe the threat to free speech is global and extends far beyond American higher education, we can nonetheless learn a great deal from what is happening on American campuses. American higher education is immensely influential and, perversely, has been on the cutting edge of censorship and other illiberal trends for decades. Therefore, examining campus attitudes about both free speech and freedom from speech may offer a preview of what the world will look like in 10 to 20 years. Also, since higher education may offer our best hope of fighting the calls for freedom from speech, it is important to see how uninterested most campuses are in helping solve the problem. In fact, they are often making it worse.

In *Unlearning Liberty* and in my other writings, I have examined how higher education pioneered the idea that some students, professors, or administrators have the "right not to be offended." This mythical right manifests itself in campus speech codes that ban "hurtful," "inconsiderate," or "offensive" speech, as well as in the kind of absurd overreactions to and punishments of speech that we see on a daily basis at FIRE. I am sad to report that since *Unlearning Liberty* was published, the bar for what can get you in trouble in college appears to have sunk even lower.

Constitution Day (which is honored yearly on Sept. 17) in 2013 was a particularly bad day for free speech on campus. At Modesto Junior College in California, student and decorated military veteran Robert Van Tuinen was told that he could not hand out copies of the U.S. Constitution to his fellow students. On the same day, at California's Citrus College, student Vincenzo Sinapi-Riddle was informed that he could not freely protest the National Security Agency (NSA) and its surveillance program on campus. Both students were required to restrict their protests to tiny "free speech zones" and had to get advance administrative permission before conducting them. Four months later, another group of students at the University of Hawaii at Hilo were told that they could not distribute copies of the Constitution to their schoolmates. (FIRE, with the help of attorneys from the national law firm Davis Wright Tremaine, filed suit against all three colleges.)

In June 2014, students at the University of Chicago got together to sign a petition against well-known gay-rights advocate and sex columnist Dan Savage for uttering the word *tranny* – an abbreviation for *transsexual* that is often used as an epithet – during a panel discussion at the school. Although Savage was arguing for the reclamation of this word as a tool of empowerment, his use of it did not sit well with some. One student argued that Savage should not be allowed to say the "T-slur" (the student refused to use the actual word) no matter what the context, and like-minded students petitioned the University of Chicago's Institute of Politics to implement a ban on "hate speech" at future lectures (an effort that the institute fortunately rejected).

But the campus-speech story that received the most media attention was doubtlessly "disinvitation season 2014," when college speaker after college speaker faced disinvitation efforts from students and faculty alike. While many were rightly outraged when such efforts were successfully directed at famous conservatives and libertarians like Condoleezza Rice, Charles Murray, and Ayaan Hirsi Ali, the public has become sadly accustomed to intolerance for conservative voices on campus. The public took greater notice, however, when the disinvitation efforts were successfully directed at former University of California, Berkeley, Chancellor Robert Birgeneau and International Monetary Fund head Christine Lagarde, both of whom are high-profile figures and neither of whom is conservative.

The term *disinvitation season* has been something of a dark joke within FIRE for years –

> *A society in which people can avoid physical pain comparatively easily will produce people who are less prepared to deal with it.*

one that has grown less funny with each passing year. FIRE has been loosely tracking some of these incidents for about a decade, but we decided in May 2014 that we needed to engage in more systematic research. While we are under no illusion that we have identified every disinvitation effort that has taken place since the turn of the century (please contact us at disinvitation@thefire.org if you know of additional examples), we have compiled an extensive database of examples of disinvitation efforts over the past 15 years.

So far, FIRE has uncovered 257 incidents since 2000 in which students or faculty have pushed for speakers who were invited to campus (for both commencement and other speaking engagements) to be disinvited. Of those incidents, 111 were "successful," in that the speaker ultimately did not give a speech. Those 111 successful disinvitations took three main forms: 75 occurred via the revocation of the speaker's invitation to campus; 20 were from speakers withdrawing in the face of protest; and 16 were "heckler's vetoes," in which speakers were shouted down, chased off stage, or otherwise prevented from delivering their remarks by student hecklers.

Although these 257 disinvitation efforts span 15 years, more than half (137) have happened since 2009, when we first noticed an uptick in the frequency of such incidents. And of the 111 "successful" disinvitation attempts, 59 occurred during or after 2009. The available data strongly indicates that the problem is only getting worse; the past 5 ½ years have already seen more attempts at disinvitations, and more successful disinvitations, than the nine years preceding them.

There is, unsurprisingly, a clear political trend in the likelihood that a speaker will face a disinvitation attempt. Speakers are far more likely to encounter such efforts from opponents to their political left than from those to their right. Since 2000, those pushing for disinvitation targeted speakers with views more conservative than their own nearly twice as frequently (118 attempts) as they targeted speakers with views more liberal than their own (61 attempts).

The fact that conservatives are the focus of so many disinvitation efforts is made far more striking by the fact that – especially when it comes to commencement addresses – conservatives are *far* less likely to be invited to deliver speeches in the first place. According to research from Harry Enten at the polling aggregation website and blog FiveThirtyEight, in the 2013 and 2014 commencement seasons, *not a single* Republican political figure was invited to speak at the commencements of any of the top 30 universities or top 30 liberal-arts universities. In contrast, 25 Democratic political figures spoke at those same schools' commencements, ii of whom gave the main address.

Enten noted, "In an increasingly polarized political atmosphere, the current lack of Republican commencement speakers at top universities and colleges makes a lot of sense; a decent number of people, including Democrats, don't like to hear differing views." The underlying assumption here is quite disheartening. In an academic environment in which students were properly trained, one would hope the community would not only tolerate opinions with which they disagree but would also actively seek them out, as curious, creative, and disciplined minds should be taught to do. Instead, we have come to accept the reality of an academic environment in which students crave freedom from speech and from speakers with whom they disagree. We can and should expect better.

I am not alone in thinking this. The disinvitation problem has become severe enough that both William Bowen, the former president of Princeton University, and Michael Bloomberg, the Independent former mayor of New York City, scolded students for their arrogance and closed-mindedness in their 2014 commencement addresses. Bowen, who replaced the disinvited Chancellor Birgeneau as Haverford College's graduation speaker, decried the agitators' approach as "immature" and "arrogant" and called Birgeneau's disinvitation a "defeat" for the school. Bloomberg, for his part, used his commencement address to warn Harvard graduates that "tolerance for other people's ideas and the freedom to express your own are … perpetually vulnerable to the tyrannical tendencies of monarchs, mobs, and majorities, and lately we've seen those tendencies manifest themselves too often, both on college campuses and in our society."

As an attorney who focuses on free speech and the First Amendment, I fully support the rights of faculty and students to make their opinions known about a university's decision to invite any speaker. That being said, freedom of speech and academic freedom depend on our ability to handle hearing opinions we dislike and to engage those opinions constructively and creatively. Free inquiry and academic freedom, in particular, require some amount of epistemic humility and a willingness to acknowledge that even the opinion or person we find the most abhorrent might reveal some portion of the truth of which we are unaware. It is also important to recognize that even if a speaker *does* happen to be entirely wrong, we might learn more about our own beliefs or about the complex relationships among beliefs by allowing that person to speak.

Rather than teaching students to be skeptical of confirmation bias, we appear to be teaching them to have an expectation of confirmation: a sense of entitlement to an environment in which their beliefs are not contradicted (at least not too harshly). Expectation of confirmation is yet another manifestation of the desire for intellectual comfort, and it is also likely to increase over time. If we don't fight the growth of this expectation among students, we can be confident that disinvitation season will get worse and worse every year, until universities decide that the only people they can safely invite to speak will be those who have nothing to say. Still worse, catering to this expectation plays into an unhealthy narrative – that hearing from only those with whom you agree is somehow a laudable goal, rather than poison to intellectual growth.

Disinvitation season, thanks in part to its intersection with celebrities and public figures, may be the most high-profile symptom of campus illiberalism, but it isn't the only campus trend to catch the public's notice in recent months. The push for "trigger warnings" has also received considerable attention, and it may have even darker implications for the future of free and open discourse and debate.

Impossible Expectations: Trigger Warnings

In May 2014, the *New York Times* called attention to a new arrival on the college campus: trigger warnings. Seemingly overnight, colleges and universities across America have begun fielding student demands that their professors issue content warnings before covering any material that might evoke a negative emotional response. By way of illustration, the *Times* article (titled "Warning: The Literary Canon Could Make Students Squirm") pointed to a Rutgers student's op-ed requesting trigger warnings for *The Great Gatsby*, which apparently "possesses a variety of scenes that reference gory, abusive and misogynistic violence," and *Mrs. Dalloway*, which the student called "a disturbing narrative" that discusses "suicidal inclinations" and "post-traumatic experiences." The article generated significant discussion, with readers questioning why college students would need trigger warnings – which are generally billed as a way to help those who suffer from post-traumatic stress disorder (PTSD), a serious mental-health condition – before reading the type of material that any college student should expect to encounter on any college campus.

The *New Republic*'s Jenny Jarvie has traced the genesis of trigger warnings to online chat rooms and message boards frequented by survivors of highly traumatizing experiences like rape. In her March 2014 article "Trigger Happy," Jarvie noted that the warnings, which "began as a way of moderating Internet forums for the vulnerable and mentally ill," spread through feminist forums like wildfire, prompting writer Susannah Breslin to proclaim in April 2010 that feminists were using the term "like a Southern cook applies Pam cooking spray to an overused nonstick frying pan." From there, the phenomenon mushroomed into a staggeringly broad advisory system that, as Jarvie explained, now covers "topics as diverse as sex, pregnancy, addiction, bullying, suicide, sizeism, ableism, homophobia, transphobia, slut shaming, victim-blaming, alcohol, blood, insects, small holes, and animals in wigs." In May 2012, the *Awl*'s Choire Sicha penned an article titled "When 'Trigger Warning' Lost All Its Meaning." In it, Sicha discussed "how far afield 'trigger warnings' have gone," calling the trend "insulting" and "infantilizing."

Despite such criticism, trigger warnings are gaining traction – and are no longer confined to Internet forums. The leap from online communities to college campuses is not surprising, as campuses have long been at the vanguard of accommodating student, faculty, and administrator demands for emotionally and intellectually comfortable environments. Indeed, while serving as president of Barnard College, Judith Shapiro went so far as to tell faculty members "that she thought no Barnard student should be uncomfortable in any class." Shapiro's comment highlights the current collision of visions regarding the role that a college should take. Some believe that campuses have a duty to shield students from difficult material, while others espouse the older view, popularized by colleges like Yale in the 1970s, that colleges should be places where students are encouraged to "think the unthinkable, discuss the unmentionable, and challenge the unchallengeable." This contrast is stark and has certainly unsettled many professors.

In early 2014, Oberlin University took a dramatic step toward heightening students' intellectual comfort by posting a trigger-warning policy on its website. Although the policy did not mandate the use of trigger warnings, it heavily encouraged the faculty to employ them as a means of "making classrooms safer."

It is crucial, at this point, to note how thoroughly the definition of *safety* has been watered down on campus. The term is no longer limited to physical security – far from it. In my career, I have repeatedly seen *safety* be conflated with *comfort* or even *reassurance*. It is hard for me to overemphasize how dangerous this shift is. Our society appears to have forgotten the moral of the fable "The

Boy Who Cried Wolf." When there is confusion as to whether *safety* refers to physical harm or to mere discomfort, how can professors and administrators quickly assess the danger of a situation and make appropriate decisions to safeguard the physical security of their students? Making sure that such

The idea that we can truly tackle hard issues while remaining universally inoffensive – an impossible pipe dream even if it were desirable – seems to be growing increasingly popular.

important words do not lose their meaning through inappropriately distorted usage is an essential part of fighting the movement toward freedom from speech.

Oberlin's policy – which was quickly tabled

when panicked professors found out about it – shows how expansive and invasive trigger warnings can be. Its stated purpose was to protect students suffering from PTSD due to sexual assault, but its list of potentially triggering topics extended far beyond sexual or physical abuse. Professors were asked to "understand that sexual misconduct is inextricably tied to issues of privilege and oppression" and to therefore consider how topics like "racism, classism, sexism, heterosexism, cissexism, ableism, and other issues of privilege and oppression" could affect their students.

The breadth of this list reveals that trigger-warning policies often have little to do with the needs of actual PTSD sufferers. Bear in mind that PTSD is the current evolution of the term "shell shock," which was developed after World War I to describe long-term psychological harm due to sustained exposure to horrific experiences during wartime. In the 1970s, PTSD became the preferred term for referring to traumatized veterans of the Vietnam War. The term has tremendous emotional force, but its use in the trigger-warning debate is yet another troubling employment of an important word. What colleges like Oberlin describe as PTSD bears little resemblance to its original meaning, which focused on the results of exposure to severe and often prolonged physical violence, atrocities, or other life-threatening or terrifying events. Survivors of sexual assault have experienced the type of trauma that fits this definition, but it is hard to see how people who have merely been exposed to "classism" – something that virtually anyone can claim to have encountered in some way at some point – can be put in the same category.

Oberlin is not alone. Around the time that Oberlin was instituting its trigger-warning policy, the student government at the University of California, Santa Barbara, (UCSB) passed a "Resolution to Mandate Warnings for Triggering Content in Academic Settings," which the UCSB administration is currently in the process of implementing. The resolution provides a "suggested list of Trigger Warnings [that] includes Rape, Sexual Assault, Abuse, Self-Injurious Behavior, Suicide, Graphic Violence, Pornography, Kidnapping, and Graphic Depictions of Gore."

Bailey Loverin, the student who co-authored the UCSB resolution, was inspired to do so after watching a film depicting rape in class. Although she identifies as a survivor of sexual abuse, she has specifically stated that she "was not triggered by [her] classroom experience." Rather, she found it "disturbing and sickening." In other words, she felt highly uncomfortable while watching the film. Her discomfort – and her worries about the emotional comfort of her classmates – culminated in the passage of a policy that will likely force all UCSB professors to scour their course materials for anything that might be upsetting to students. The rules of political correctness seem to counsel against responding with the real answer: that college is where you are supposed to learn about the world as it truly is, which includes covering some horrific and dreadful topics. This endeavor should make anyone with a conscience uncomfortable at times, but that discomfort is a necessary part of real, adult-level education.

A quick look at recent campus dustups gives a more complete understanding of what the results of trigger-warning policies will be. In February 2014, students at Wellesley College were outraged when an artist placed a statue of a man sleepwalking in his underwear on campus. There is nothing overtly sexual or threatening about the statue, which was erected as part of a sculpture exhibit. If anything, the sleepwalker seems vulnerable: his eyes are closed, he is unaware of his surroundings, and he is barely dressed. Despite this, students called it "a source of apprehension, fear, and triggering thoughts regarding sexual assault for many members of our campus community" in a Change.org petition seeking its removal.

One of the most powerful aspects of art is its capacity to provoke thought and debate, often by raising some hackles. Yet Zoe Magid, who started the petition, asserted that artwork that makes people uncomfortable has no place at Wellesley: "We really feel that if a piece of art makes students feel unsafe, that steps over a line." Make sure to note how *unsafe* is used in this context.

At UCSB (again), a professor used the idea of triggers to defend getting into a physical altercation with campus protesters. In March 2014, Mireille Miller-Young, a UCSB feminist-studies professor, spotted a young woman carrying a pro-life sign that displayed images of aborted fetuses. She tore the sign from the activist's hands and went so far as to shove another protester who tried to retrieve it. When questioned by the UCSB Police Department, Miller-Young – who was pregnant at the time – declared that "she felt 'triggered' by the images on the poster." She also portrayed herself as a defender of student comfort, claiming that "other students in the area were 'triggered' in a negative way by their imagery." In other words, she placed greater value on the emotional comfort of those with whom she identified than on the physical security of the women she assaulted. In the video of the incident, Miller-Young seems positively gleeful to have taken the protesters' signs, and her actions make her argument that she was personally triggered, as opposed to simply angry, difficult to believe. That defense appears to be little more than a post hoc way of making her seem more sympathetic.

It is easy to dismiss events like that as rare acts of lunacy. One can argue that Miller-Young was just a lone professor making a transparent attempt to garner sympathy for – or otherwise excuse – illegal behavior. It is also easy to dismiss the rising popularity of trigger warnings as a flash in the pan that will fade in the face of public ridicule. Yet the policies and confrontations that stem from the concept of trigger warnings are just further symptoms of the increasing expectations of intellectual comfort and freedom from speech on campus. While it is possible that the particular problem of demands for trigger warnings will be short-lived (though I doubt it), there will persist a larger problem of a limitless "care ethic" in which outsiders are responsible for safeguarding the emotional state of all, even at the risk of impeding discourse on dead-serious topics that must be explored.

The UCSB case also highlights how such policies will inevitably be abused. An unfortunate truth of human nature is that if we are given a cudgel that may be wielded against people and views we oppose, some of us will gladly swing it. I can say with near 100 percent confidence that students and even other faculty members will use trigger rationales to silence voices on campus that they merely dislike.

And professors know it is already shockingly easy to get in trouble for what you say at today's colleges. Take the 2014 example of art instructor Francis Schmidt of Bergen Community College in New Jersey, who was suspended without pay and ordered to undergo psychological counseling for posting on

Google Plus a picture of his daughter wearing a T-shirt featuring a quote from the warrior queen Daenerys Targaryen, a character on HBO's mega-hit *Game of Thrones.* "I will take what is mine with fire and blood." Depressingly, the quote was interpreted by administrators as a serious threat of violence. A security official even claimed that the "fire" reference could be a proxy for the gunfire of an AK-47. A strikingly similar case, this time involving a quote from the sci-fi cult television classic *Firefly*, took place at the University of Wisconsin-Stout in 2011.

An unfortunate truth of human nature is that if we are given a cudgel that may be wielded against people and views we oppose, some of us will gladly swing it.

Broaching sex-related topics in the classroom can be particularly risky, with professors at Appalachian State University; the University of Colorado, Boulder; and the University of Denver all facing harassment charges and removal from teaching for the inclusion of sexual content in their class materials and discussions, even though the content was demonstrably relevant to each course.

In an environment like this, imposing on professors the duty to anticipate and be responsible for their students' emotional reactions to material will simply create new rationales for students or administrators seeking to punish provocative instructors. Such an expectation would be disastrous for teaching and would place professors in an impossible position.

Oberlin Professor Marc Blecher has pointed out that instructors without tenure would be particularly vulnerable to this effect, telling the *New York Times*, "If I were a junior faculty member looking at this [the Oberlin policy] while putting my syllabus together, I'd be terrified." In May 2014, seven humanities professors from seven colleges penned an *Inside Higher Ed* article stating that "this movement is already having a chilling effect on [their] teaching and pedagogy." They reported receiving "phone calls from deans and other administrators investigating student complaints that they have included 'triggering' material in their courses, with or without warnings." Sometime in the not-so-distant future – if it has not happened already – professors *will* be punished for not providing a trigger warning before discussing material that a student finds objectionable.

The seven professors also raised an important point about how trigger-warning policies may well harm, rather than help, the very students they claim to protect: "Trigger warnings may encourage students to file claims against faculty rather than seek support and resources for debilitating reactions to stressors." Students with PTSD are suffering from a serious mental-health condition and should seek professional assistance for it.

In her article "Treatment, Not Trigger Warnings," Sarah Roff, a psychiatrist who specializes in the mental effects of trauma (including flashbacks and panic attacks), explained that training students to avoid certain topics can be quite detrimental:

> One of the cardinal symptoms of PTSD is avoidance, which can become the most impairing symptom of all. If someone has been so affected by an event in her life that reading a description of a rape in Ovid's Metamorphoses *can trigger* nightmares, flashbacks, and panic attacks, she is likely to be functionally impaired in areas of her life well beyond the classroom. The solution is not to help these students dig themselves further into a life of fear and avoidance.

Proponents of trigger warnings argue that safeguarding the comfort of traumatized students is well worth the potential costs. Their position holds great emotional appeal. In the words of Shakesville's Melissa McEwan, a leading trigger-warning advocate, "We provide trigger warnings because it's polite, because we don't want to be the asshole who triggered a survivor of sexual assault because of carelessness or laziness or ignorance." The vast majority of us don't want to hurt others, particularly those who have already been badly hurt.

This emotional appeal can serve as a formidable weapon, especially as Haidt's care ethic becomes unbound from other moral or practical considerations. Those who oppose trigger warnings are accused of being insensitive to the needs of vulnerable groups. It is also considered illegitimate to question the sincerity of emotional responses, which makes it easy for students who dislike certain ideas (or individuals) to try to silence them by claiming to have been triggered by them. Casting doubt on such an assertion would constitute "victim blaming," which only a coldhearted monster would do. Alleging that someone is insensitive to the emotional state of victims is a powerful and effective shortcut to taking the moral high ground in contemporary debate.

The fear of being demonized in this manner is justified, given the power of the modern "Twitter mob" and other manifestations of popular outrage. In fact, such concerns are particularly valid on campus, where professors rightfully fear for their jobs if they manage to spark the moral indignation of some subset of students, administrators, or faculty members. It is for this reason that groups that fight for

Trigger warnings starkly reinforce the mentality that demands freedom from *speech.*

professors' rights, such as FIRE and the American Association of University Professors, must do their best to bolster professorial resistance to new and impossible expectations like trigger warnings. Otherwise, we risk squandering the opportunity to work with our natural allies (in this case at least) – university professors –

to oppose the push toward elevating intellectual comfort over intellectual growth.

In rereading the commentary and reactions to the *Times* article that I mentioned at the beginning of this chapter, I noticed that defenders of trigger warnings often struck a common note. Essentially, they argued, "What's the big deal? So you have to include two little words before you cover emotionally difficult material. Is it really that much to ask?" I have offered various answers to that question throughout this Broadside, but in conclusion, I want to stress two of them. First, the trouble with trigger warnings lies less in the individual practice (although it will present a huge problem for teaching) than in what that practice represents. Trigger warnings starkly reinforce the mentality that demands freedom *from* speech. Second, the trigger-warning issue is a genuinely slippery slope, as Oberlin's staggeringly broad policy demonstrates.

Supporters of trigger warnings are sometimes shocked by the negative response that the idea, as applied to college content, has received in the press and blogosphere. For those who believe that Haidt's care ethic is paramount and that offering such warnings is simply a means of showing empathy, conscientiousness, and care, the widespread criticism of the practice is probably fairly mystifying. To those who value intellectual freedom, however, trigger warnings are yet another manifestation of the attitude that society must protect every individual from emotionally difficult speech. It is impossible to live up to this expectation, and in the course of trying to do so, we risk devastating freedom of speech and the open exchange of ideas.

Critics might dismiss my and others' concerns about what trigger warnings represent as a slippery-slope fallacy. But if there is one thing that I have discovered in fighting for free speech on campus, it is that when it comes to limitations on speech and the uniquely sensitive environment of college campuses, the slope is genuinely perilously slick.

In my career, I have seen harassment rationales – meant to prevent misogynists from forcing women out of jobs through constant abuse – being invoked to justify censoring everything from quoting popular television shows to faintly implying criticism of a university's hockey coach to publicly reading a book. The slippery slope of censorship is demonstrably not a fallacy on campus. When students take advantage of a psychological term developed to help those traumatized in the ghastly trenches of World War I justify being protected from *The Great Gatsby*, sleepwalker statues, and, as the Oberlin policy specified, Chinua Achebe, it becomes clear that there is virtually no limit to the demands that will be made if we universalize an expectation of intellectual comfort.

Other critics see where this is headed, as well. As Professor Roff wrote in the article mentioned above, "since triggers are a contagious phenomenon, there will never be enough trigger warnings to keep up with them." And as Conor Friedersdorf wrote in the *Atlantic*:

The future before us if the most sweeping plans for "trigger warnings" become reality, is a kind of arms race, where different groups of students demand that their highly particular, politicized sensitivities are as deserving of a trigger warning as any other. Everyone from anarchists to college Republicans will join in. Kids will feel trauma when their trauma isn't recognized as trauma. "Trigger warnings" will be as common and useless as "adult content" warnings on HBO.

Everyone will be worse off.

Friedersdorf is right. The "offendedness sweepstakes" (to borrow a phrase from Rauch) pushes the bar ever lower for what is deemed unacceptably offensive, while the realm of unacceptable speech grows ever larger. This is a global race to the bottom, and it is being run most fiercely in higher education. In the process, candor, discussion, humor, honest dialogue, and freedom of speech are imperiled.

Conclusion: Fighting the Problems of Comfort

My primary goal in this short work has been to explain that threats to free speech, while rampant on college campuses, are not unique to higher education or even to the United States, and why we can expect them to intensify over time. I have also offered a preview of where I fear we are headed. While this view may strike some as unduly pessimistic, I think it is necessary to correctly diagnose the problem if we are sincere about tackling it.

If I am right, and the move toward greater physical, emotional, and intellectual comfort is a predictable historical force, understanding what is coming may help us prepare for it. My fear is that future generations will not see much point in delving into emotionally difficult topics and that those of us who argue that doing so is intellectually "good for you" will sound a lot like parents telling stubborn children that they should eat their Brussels sprouts.

I am constantly on the lookout for potential cures for this problem. Litigation plays an important role in the fight, as does having students engage in proper Oxford-style debates (like we see today in the Intelligence Squared series). Comedians and satirists may also join the pushback against the infinite care ethic; after all, it is blazingly clear that politically correct censorship and comedy are natural enemies. And, of course, nothing can replace teaching students at every level of education

---

It is blazingly clear that politically correct censorship and comedy are natural enemies.

---

the old-fashioned intellectual habits of epistemic humility, giving others the benefit of the doubt, and actually listening to opposing opinions. Such practices need to make a comeback if we are to have a society in which it is at all productive (let alone pleasurable) to talk about anything serious.

I hope to write extensively in the coming years about the potential solutions to problems of comfort, the expectation of confirmation, and the desire for freedom from speech. But unless higher education stops encouraging these inclinations and starts combating them, it will be a hard battle indeed.

Then again, the fight for freedom of speech has never been easy.

First American edition published in 2014 by Encounter Books,
an activity of Encounter for Culture and Education, Inc.,
a nonprofit, tax exempt corporation.
Encounter Books website address: www.encounterbooks.com

Manufactured in the United States and printed on
acid-free paper. The paper used in this publication meets
the minimum requirements of ANSI/NISO Z39.48–1992
(R 1997) (*Permanence of Paper*).

FIRST AMERICAN EDITION

LIBRARY OF CONGRESS
CATALOGING-IN-PUBLICATION DATA
IS AVAILABLE

ISBN: 978-1-59403-807-5
ISBN (EBOOK): 978-1-59403-808-2

10 9 8 7 6 5 4 3 2 1